# Conscious Wellbeing

## How to create a meaningful life
## IN THE WORKPLACE

Written By
# SONITRA SUE SINGH

WOW Book Publishing™

Conscious Wellbeing:
How to create a meaningful life
IN THE WORKPLACE

First Edition Published by Sonitra Sue Singh

Copyright date © December 2019 Sonitra Sue Singh

WOW Book Publishing™

ISBN: 9781670634825

The purpose of this book is to educate and entertain.
The views and opinions expressed in this book are that
of the author based on her personal experiences and
education. The author does not guarantee that anyone
following the techniques, suggestions, ideas or strategies
will become successful.

The author shall neither be liable nor responsible for any
loss or damage allegedly arising from any information or
suggestion in this book.

# DEDICATION

I dedicate this book to all my colleagues that I worked with over the years who taught me to be the best that I can be as a nurse.

I dedicate this book to all my patients and their relatives who allowed me to learn so much through caring for them.

I dedicate this book to my mom Kalawathee Singh and my late dad Lall Singh who gave me this life and set me free to lead my life at my own free will.

Their gifts ultimately lead to me writing this book so that I can serve you through this book.

# TABLE OF CONTENTS

## Section A
## THE MIND

## Section B
## WEALTH

# FOREWORD

*C*onscious *Wellbeing* is the book you need to read if you are searching for a meaningful work life. Written by award-winning nursing teacher, Sonitra Singh, (who is an amasing person) this book contains a world-transformative vision and invaluable experience in creating a meaningful work life.

Despite being written for hospital staff, Conscious Wellbeing identifies the common challenges we all face at work and successfully presents helpful ideas and tips on how to enjoy a meaningful life at work. The information in this book has the power to transform your life and improve your perspective on your work and colleagues.

Sonitra has gained years of experience and skills from caring for royals, celebrities, and the common man. From my interactions with her, it is clear to me that, through this book, she has the willingness to transform your life and make the workplace a better place to be.

*—Vishal Morjaria*
*Award Winning Author and*
*International Speaker*

# TESTIMONIALS

*Conscious wellbeing* is the book you need to read if you searching for a meaningful life at work. Despite this book is written for hospital staff in mind but Sue has identified the common challenges we all face at work and has successfully given us great ideas and tips to enjoy a meaningful life at work.

*—Vinogan Moodley*
*Accountant – USA*

As a Nurse Educator, I found this book perfect for all healthcare professionals. It will reflect to the reader how mindfulness overcome the challenges in clinical practice. A highly recommended piece of reading that will lead to a healthy mind and soul.

*—Michael Canete*
*Nurse Educator (iTraining Ltd)*
*Senior Lecturer (Kingston &*
*St Georges University of London)*

Sue has written a fantastic book. The information in this book has the power to transform your work life.

*—Ruveer Ramdhani*
*Chemical Engineer*
*JHB -South Africa*

I can inform you from my interaction with Sue that she has a vast amount of years of experience, skills and knowledge obtained from looking after people of all categories which she brings through in this book. She has the willingness to transform your life and make the workplace a better place to be.

*—Milda Poderiene*
*Senior Nursing Sister*
*Northwest University Healthcare*
*NHS Trust – United Kingdom*

A delightful book to read that gives insight and information on how to apply a complete awareness of the effect that your actions have on you as well as on others

*—Evalyn Tan*
*Recovery Team Manager*
*Operating Theatre – United Kingdom*

Sue has been so helpful. I know you will get a lot of help from reading this book. There is a lot of information here that I can use as a teacher for myself and my students.

*—Vienasa Nundlall*
*Senior Teacher*
*South Africa*

I travelled with Sue on her tours to India and Nepal. She is so knowledgeable. I know you will love her book. Please read her book.

*—Satrani Mahadeo*
*Retired ITU Sister*
*United Kingdom*

I have known Sue for a long time. She has written a fantastic book. Well written tips and ideas to help you with stress management. Easy to read and easy to apply.

*—Dr Munita Grover*
*ITU Consultant*
*London Northwest University*
*Healthcare NHS Trust*

I have known Sue for a long time. Her unique knowledge on this subject is well written and explained.

*Fiona Murphy MBE*
*Associate Director of Nursing*
*End of Life, Bereavement,*
*Organ and Tissue Donation*
*Northern Care Alliance*

# ACKNOWLEDGEMENT

I thank my intimate circle of friends & confidantes Evalyn Tan, Michael Canete and Tita Martel , my go to people who keep me grounded and centred and keep reminding me that I have the potential to write. Thank you Michael Canete for being a great mentor and developing my teaching skills. Through teaching, I realized my writing skills.

I acknowledge my Spiritual Family who continuously guide & inspire me with spiritual insights. HH Jayapataka Swami (my Guru), Brajavilas Das, Praghosa Das, Citralekha dd (from Sweden) today I can see and experience the world through spiritual eyes.

Thank you to My dearest and generous Mom - Kalawathee Singh who set me free to travel the world and learn which has helped me now to pen down my learning to share with the world. I am deeply grateful to Jiovaan Chetty (my nephew) who has been my guiding support on this book journey. To my cousins Vienasa Nundlall and Prema Madhurya Dasi who are my forever cheerleaders when I most need you. Thank you to my brother Shamir and my sister Sharmain for always being there for me.

I acknowledge the great teachers and leaders of the world for making the world a better place to live and inspiring me through their actions. Her Majesty the Queen, President Nelson Mandela, Prime Minister Narendra Modi, Mahatma Gandhi, Sir Richard Branson, Deepak Chopra & Oprah Winfrey—whom I did many courses with, Anthony Robbins—whom I did many courses with, Jay Shetty, Betty Shine, Louise Hay.

Vishal Morjaria—for teaching me how to write a book and giving me the confidence and platform to do so, Shilpa Shetty, Priyanka Chopra , Twinkle Khanna – who are perfect role models in many ways, Chef Vicky Ratnani— thank you for educating me on all things food, cooking and food shopping.

I thank all my patients and their relatives for being part of my work journey. Thank you for allowing me to learn so much through caring for you. I acknowledge the Lord and higher powers for blessing me with this opportunity. Finally, I acknowledge you for receiving this book and using it appropriately for your wellbeing.

# THE ARTWORK
# EXPLAINED -
# ABOUT THE
# BOOK COVER

I specifically chose the lotus flower for my book cover. The lotus flower despite being born in murky muddy water where hope for life seems almost impossible it still manages to survive the adverse condition and blooms producing a beautiful brightly coloured flower.

If you observe closely you will see as the lotus opens, not a drop of mud or dirt from the surrounding murky water can be seen entering the external petals yet it is the same muddy water that washes it clean.

The lotus represents awakening. It may appear fragile when you touch it but it is strong and tightly secured by its stem which teaches us the importance of keeping our core strong so we can withstand anything. The following are lessons we can learn from the lotus flower:

1. Compassion

2. Love

3. Hope

4. Forgiveness

Let us awaken like the lotus flower full of hope and compassion without taking on any negativity we have picked up from all that we were exposed to in our darkest hours of unknowingly.

# ABOUT THE AUTHOR

Sonitra Sue Singh (better known as Sue to her patients and colleagues) is a Registered Nurse & Midwife, Nurse Educator, and Registered Intensive Care Nurse with over 30 years of Intensive Care experience.

Sonitra is an ISKCON initiated devotee of HH Jayapataka Swami and he gave her the Spiritual name of Sukanti Radha Devi Dasi meaning " the effulgence of Radharani." Sue studied several Vedic literature at the ISKCON London Temple in Soho Street in United Kingdom. Her favourite book is the Bhagavad Gita.

She is currently serving ISKCON as the UK-Europe fundraising co ordinator in helping to build the Temple of Vedic Planetarium (TOVP) which when completed will be the largest Hindu temple in the world located in Kolkata - India. You can find more info on that on www.tovp. org. Sonitra was born in South Africa and lives in UK where she practices as an Intensive Care Nurse in London.

She has a great interest in Energy & Vibrational medicine involving hands on healing and received initiation as a Reiki Master in 1999 in London. Her interest in alternative medicine led her to travel to Kerala and study Ayurveda where she obtained qualification as a Panchakarma Ayurvedic Practitioner. For the past 20 years, Sonitra has been organising small tours to India and teaches personal development courses.

Her favourite amongst most of her travellers are the Tours to Mayapur which is in the City of Kolkata and the Golden Triangle Tour in India. She also works with doctors and nurses in India organising medical camps and takes small groups to India as volunteers as time permits. With her wide variety of knowledge and skill Sonitra has nursed many members of the Royal families from around the world including UK, Qatar, Saudi Arabia and members of the Royal Zulu family in South Africa.

Her clients also include several VIP's, MP's and celebrities of Hollywood and Bollywood. Currently, Sonitra is teaching several nursing clinical courses including End of Life Care and Well-being courses in London. More information is available on her social media.

# Section A
# THE MIND

*"If you have a strong mind and plant in it a strong resolve, you can change your destiny"*

—Paramahansa Yogananda

# Chapter 1

# MIND CONSCIOUSNESS

## *What is My Life Purpose?*

Our life is a precious gift. When we receive a precious gift then it's our duty to take care of it to the best of our ability. We often ask our self the question: what is my real purpose on this earth? Or if we on the path we are meant to trodden on? Or am I on the right career? We are curious about what our journey is going to be like. It is normal human nature to be curious. When we curious, we expand our consciousness. Your true worth lies within you. It is waiting to be utilised.

Work is a journey. It is a journey where we can learn many things about ourselves. Everyone is born with a unique journey. It is important for us to know our life's true journey and stay on that path. If we do not know our journey then we end up either copying other people's journey or we find ourselves lost in this world. When we take other peoples journey then we always end up at crossroads. At crossroads, there are many directions. If the person whose journey we have copied is not with us at the crossroad then we might take the wrong turn. Coming back to our own path then might take a longer journey with all these detours but lots to learn along the way for our own personal development. Therefore, it is best to take our own journey and enjoy the ride.

You are on the driver's seat of your own journey. You have all the controls at your side. So why do we have to give the controls to someone else to take us on their journey which might be the wrong path for us to follow. No two people can go through the exact experience in life. It would then be ridiculous to compare ourselves to someone or any two people. Whatever you take birth to deliver in this world is your life purpose and no one can take that away from you. Your journey could be something that you need to either learn from, something you need to complete in this lifetime, or something you need to support. Only you know what your role is for that moment of time. Only you can unfold that purpose by being present at all times to observe the clues that come your way. By knowing and understanding your life's purpose will help you to stay in the flow of things and make life more meaningful.

When life is meaningful then it reduces stress in the workplace. Because everything is happening the way it is meant to be. If we concentrate on our inner talents and give our best to what we enjoy doing then we can be reassured that we achieving our life's purpose.

Look at some of our domestic cleaners at our hospitals. Some of them look so happy in their job as if they are in deep meditation while working. Yet some are degree holders and highly qualified in their own respective countries. Yet they humbly go about their task. They have no intention for a higher post. Just happy doing what they doing. Just happy on their life purpose. When they accept that this is their life purpose then we all marvel at this sight. Work then becomes an amazing journey in a mood of serving others. Have you ever noticed on duty how when two people work together and are a space and support to each other how well they work together?

One relying on the other while the other just being present for that person in that space. If you enjoying that then you certainly fulfilling your life's purpose. If you are unable to realise your life path and the things that bring you joy then you going to be in an environment that is not suitable for your growth.

You might find yourself disturbing your colleagues around you who are seriously trying to save lives or get on with their work. Failure to notice your unhappiness can lead to stress and diseases. So the quicker you work out where you need to be and want you want to do, the easier it will be for you and those around you. The care that you will deliver thereafter will be outstanding.

When we become a nurse, we choose nursing to help heal someone. But when we get higher up the position then our goals change. We no longer want to heal, we want to lead or manage.

One can spend an awful lot of time and money chasing this upward ladder leaving behind the very purpose of coming into the career to heal. Sometimes diverting our goals can change our purpose in this life. Take time out for self-enquiry.

Enquire from yourself... -

- Who am I?

- Am I a shoulder for someone to lean on to regain their strength?

- Am I the space for someone as a support in his or her career or work life?

- What are my talents?

- What are the things I do that brings other people joy?

- What are the things that I do that enriches other people's lives?

- What am I passionate about?

As Jay Shetty says, *"**Your passion is for you and your purpose is for others**"*. The answers lie within you. Stop looking outside, look within. Find that passion. It is for you. Then use that passion to make others happy, that then is service. This is our path to conscious wellbeing.

## *Leaving a Legacy*

Leaving a legacy is like giving back to the world what the world has already given to you. Once you have found your life purpose and trodden your path, you may now want to consider helping others and leaving a legacy.

- You may want to consider how best you want to serve humanity?

- To what are you dedicating your life?

- How you want to be remembered after you die?

With this in mind whatever you do now will serve as a legacy, will help you grow into a better human being and bring out the good qualities in you that best represent you. Legacies are like pathways that guide your decisions.

It includes all that you achieve including your failures that become building blocks on your path. Nobody wants to leave a bad legacy behind. So take time out to consider what kind of legacy you would like to leave behind.

## *Mindfulness - Be Present on Your Job*

Mindfulness literally means thinking of nothing else other than what you doing right now. By being present, this allows us to be more aware of our purpose. By living in the present moment, we are attracted towards our life's purpose and the things best suited for our work journey. In order for us to function in full mode, we need to raise our vibration to the appropriate frequency then only we can channel what we want into our work life.

Just like if you need to listen to a clear radio station you need to change the dials to reach the appropriate clear radio station frequency.

When we achieve the clear station then we have attuned to the correct station.

When we to raise our vibration then we can provide the optimum care to our patients. For that, we need to be present on our job. We need to be mindful. We become aligned. The reason why we cannot be in the present moment and tend to have too much confusion or become overwhelmed by stuff is that we have too much chores or activity around us that distracts us.

We need to prioritise and ignore the rest. You only have so much attention. If you follow this, you will become less likely to confusion or being overwhelmed.

By being present, we avoid making unnecessary mistakes. Medication errors can be avoided. Infection rates can drop. When we not present our mind is somewhere else. We miss the important information.

This then opens us to make mistakes, as we are not fully focused. Some errors are human, and to err is human after all. However, to make deliberate mistakes because our mind was elsewhere is not acceptable, especially when we dealing with life. Life is precious! When we are able to make less mistakes, we suffer less mental strain.

When we are present, we are able to think clearly of all the areas of our life. In order for us to keep the practice of being mindful, we have to practice mindfulness through the process of conscious breathing. Taking time out every day will be the best investment you can give yourself. It is easy to practice being present once you get started. You need to give yourself that time to get used to the practice until it becomes second nature to you. Controlling the mind is not a easy process but taming it with the use of 10 minutes breathe control everyday helps to ease the process.

## *What Being Happy at Work Really Means?*

Happiness can mean different things for different people. Happiness is our natural state of being. When you do something that you are passionate about then that makes you happy. When you use what you passionate about to make others happy, then that's what is called service. You only need three things to be happy:

- Be the master of your mind and body; take control of your senses. Take good care of your body. Once your mind and body are in alignment and good health, then you will feel a deep feeling of peace. Health is wealth.

- Find your life purpose; is the work you doing really your life purpose?

- Do the things required in accomplishing your purpose; set your goals and work to achieve them.

Happy people carry a positive energy and are always involved in positive talk. They see the good in everything as everything is purposeful. They can laugh at themselves. They look radiant at work. They speak from their heart. They have deep gratitude and appreciative for anything that comes their way and see it as a blessing. They love doing tasks they do and expecting nothing in return. They go with the flow.

Sometimes we fail to observe such people and learn from them. It is normal human nature that we cannot always be happy especially when we not serving in our lives purpose. Many extrinsic factors can add to our unhappiness if we allow it to; this is especially true if we have not mastered the art of controlling our senses, or if we don't take time to deal with our unwanted thoughts. We have to master how to transcend this. It is very important to recognise what makes you unhappy.

Is it the procedure you doing? Is it the environment? Is it the people or some people around you? Know who your go to person or place is when you are unhappy. Observe what happens to your body when you unhappy. How does your body react? How do you feel?

Be conscious of all your feelings, thoughts and bodily reactions. When you quickly learn the clues that bring you unhappiness then consider all your options that can help you move towards your life purpose. Avoid sulking for too long. If you sulk, you sulk alone.

If you not enjoying your work then the question arises then what exactly are you doing? When we come on duty we often ask our colleagues how was their day. They will tell us either they had a good time today or that work was good today. There is a big difference in the meaning of both these answers. Having a good day means goals for the day have been set, results were achieved, and time was well spent.

This will give you a clue as to exactly what went on in that shift. Having a good time at work means you did not really get work done, you probably upset a few of your colleagues and you did not achieve really anything.

No goals were set therefore no goals achieved. As nurses, we pride ourselves with our job. But do we really get the job done? If we say we had a good day, we mean we got a lot of work done; we took the patient to CT scan, we spoke to relatives about how they were coping, we filed our patients' notes, and so on. Meaning we actually got something done. We reached our goals. So next time someone asks you how was your day. Be conscious of the fact that you want to let them know you were not having a good time at work but rather work was good today.

You achieved your goals. As a manager, you want to see results and goals achieved. Staff need to be conscious of the fact that they need to enjoy what they doing to fulfil this. This ultimately leads to a happier work place and environment. Your work then becomes more meaningful; there must be something you get out of it.

Otherwise, it becomes task oriented and you will not enjoy it. Whatever you do, you need to be happy doing and enjoy doing. Success is not the key to happiness but rather happiness is the key to success. When you happy, your body mind and soul is in a heightened form of energy. When you happy, there is no stopping you. Anything becomes achievable. Happiness does not come from having everything but rather from making the best out of what you have. It is all about how you see yourself. Happiness is not having what you like but rather liking what you have and being content with it.

## *When Work Becomes a Vocation*

A vocation is something that comes from within to do something that you are meant to do. Nursing is a vocation. Jay Shetty tells us 46% of our stress comes from workload. Twenty percent of our stress comes from balancing personal and professional life.

When your job becomes a vocation we transcend the stress of workload and become able to balance our personal and professional life because we doing what we meant to be doing. There are no must have's and must do's in vocational life. When we experience work as vocation then one can really experience the deep happiness in your heart. Your heart is full of compassion and the need to constantly give without thinking of what you getting back. We have to be 100% committed. With our kind of work, we need to be on point always. We cannot afford mistakes or wasting time. We have to be heart and soul. Then only we can enjoy what we doing from our heart. Work is a vocation when we can end our shift in joy and gratitude. Knowing you gave the best service you can without any expectation. When work becomes a vocation one naturally avoids taking heavy baggage home. That is our goal. That helps us in our road to conscious wellbeing.

## *Our Imperfect Senses*

We are humans with faults. We are born with imperfect senses. Imperfection is our human right. We are allowed to make mistakes unknowingly. Mistakes done with full knowledge and understanding is unacceptable. As humans, we have four defects:

1. Imperfect Senses – our senses are limited and can easily be misled
2. Illusion – accepting something as real that is not real
3. Mistakes – to err is human
4. Cheating – to present yourself as something you are not

When we have knowledge and full understanding of this, we can better connect and cooperate with each other fully accepting each other's shortcomings. Being aware of these defects help us to improve them so that we can be a better human being.

## *Reflective Questions*

What is the most valuable message you received in this chapter?

_____

_____

_____

What will you do different based on what you've learnt?

_____

_____

_____

How will you ensure you do what you've written above in previous question?

_____

_____

_____

What's been your light bulb moment whilst reading this chapter?

_____

_____

_____

What do you think is your life purpose?

_____

_____

_____

# *Notes*

_____

_____

_____

_____

_____

_____

_____

_____

_____

_____

_____

_____

_____

_____

_____

## Section *B*

# WEALTH

*"Wealth consists not in having great possessions, but in having few wants."*

—Epictetus

# Chapter 2
## MONEY CONSCIOUSNESS

### *Am I Working for Money?*

The big question here is "Am I working for money?" That changes everything about our wellbeing at work. According to a quote attributed to the Dalai Lama, "Man sacrifices his health in order to make money. Then he sacrifices money in order to recuperate his health" We live in a material world.

Money is important to survive in the material world. However, if we work purely for money, then we become money driven and to some extent can put our wellbeing at risk. Some people can work up to 10 days in a row without a day off. By chatting with them and hearing their stories you can immediately know that they are not looking after themselves.

What to speak of their care to other people if they cannot have self-care. In some cultures, 10% of earnings are encouraged to be used for charity. This is a good practice; it keeps you humble. It teaches you to share. It gives you the realisation that you are part of a big world and not just the immediate family in which you are born.

If you choose to donate to charity then it is important to know more of the charity you are giving to so that you know your money is being utilised for the right purposes intended. We are living at a time when money has value. So if we want something to have value, we give it a price tag. When it has a price tag then we can appreciate the value.

We get paid because we live in a material world. We have to pay our rent, buy food and take care of our families. When something is earned, it is respected. We do not work for money. Money works for us. When we attend study events, we have to pay for it. When we pay for it then we appreciate it. We attend the class with full attention for our monies worth. We are able to see the price tag.

## *Is Money Evil?*

Money in itself is good and beneficial. Money has energy. If you understand how energy works then you will know how to attract money. Having the love for money is not evil. It depends on how you use the money. In his book, Master your WOW,

Vishal Morjaria says that years of conditioning from various belief systems can lead one to believe that money is the root of all evil if you go on believing this then this will affect your wealth and your relationship with money. It will create a barrier to wealth. If money is earned for the purpose that best serves you, then that is good money.

If money is used for destructive purposes, hoarded or gambled then that can lead to diseases and loss of money too. Gambling develops greed and need to always win in a person. If we follow the path of love then we follow the path where everything comes to us as we need it. It adds to our lives. It is the path of abundance. The minute we follow the path of gambling, greed, selfishness then we open our path to poverty. If you believe in God, the universe, or the energy above, then know that that is the place of abundance. Because God, energy, or the universe is unconditional love.

When we cut ourselves from that source, then our supplies are diminished. Therefore, whatever we do, we need to do from a place of love. Then we connected to the abundance energy. There is a being higher than us with abundance so we need to tap into that energy of abundance.

It is possible that someone's shift can get cancelled due to custom rules (meaning full time staff, get booked first over part time staff). In this case, a shift leader or manager is not mindful of the bigger picture that the part time staff might be the appropriate person to be booked but rather his/her thought becomes consumed with rules and regulations and thereby book the less suited person on the shift.

The disadvantage of this decision can lead to increased workload, poor patient outcome and decreased productivity with the inappropriate person booked due to custom rules. Sometimes by thinking out of the box and out of custom rules can help us improve the quality of our work and outcome.

Sometimes some staff have to consistently do bank shifts to keep abreast of their monthly income. In his Genius video, Jay Shetty says that 31% of stress comes from conflicts of money issues and 72% of stress comes from financial difficulties. You will be surprised how many of us do not know how to manage our money. When we lose control in money management and spend beyond our means or what we budgeted for then that leads to conflicts in money issues. We develop stress.

Our imbalance takes over and we cannot balance between personal and professional life. In these circumstances what do we do? We dump it on people around us. We stress our families, our friends and our colleagues. Insecurities set in. We become money madness and this changes our behaviour.

Instead of looking around and ensuring every nurse or doctor or healthcare provider takes home a salary, we start abusing and cancelling our bank nurses and support staff in greed of their shifts. Thinking only of ourselves. Not thinking they are our support staff who are there for us in time of need. We lose our minds and stop thinking of other people's welfare.

Money greed makes us selfish. Vishal Mojaria says from his wealth research that Health, Finance, Relationships, Spirituality and Giving Back has to be balanced in order for us to achieve a happy, successful and fulfilling life. I still remember the day I did my first bank shift at a hospital. I was allocated to work with a nurse who happens to also be from South Africa. She thanked me for supporting her unit and welcomed me to it. She then humbly orientated me to the rest of the nurses. I will never forget this moment in my life. I felt so proud of her, and, even today, I thank her for her kind gesture and creating such a wonderful memory for me, a temporary staff member.

## *How Much Money Is Enough?*

In 1930, British economist John Maynard Keynes predicted that with technology change and productivity improvements would eventually lead to a 15-hour workweek as people's material needs would be satisfied. However, we still work 35–40 hour week. We have not been able to achieve this desirable prediction.

There are some people who live beyond their means or suffer a greed mentality. Some people suffer "money addiction" and do not even know that. How many times have you reflected on your bank shifts and told yourself that you have done more than you should have? That is a powerful question to ask yourself. It shows how much you value yourself, your health and your time.

Have you ever cancelled a bank shift because you did too many? If you have then you need to pat yourself on the back for taking care of yourself. Too many times senior staff may approach you and encourage you to work and may say things like "work while you still young" or "get the shift done as in the summer there won't be bank shifts".

They tend to cover their own shifts or cover the unit without considering the impact on your health. They may approach you with good intentions, but it's up to you to decide what is in your best interest. You should always serve yourself first. Look after your body and mind first before giving yourself to serve others. You cannot go to work and give off your best if you yourself need wellbeing support.

## *Is Money Overtaking Other Priorities?*

It is important to sit down and list your priorities. Make the list from high priority to low priority. Priorities differ for different people. Spending time with family, loved ones, and oneself is of utmost importance to some, while others need to be alone or with their pets or nature.

If these are your priorities then when you have to choose between a shift and your priority then what do you choose? Because we all place our patients first, hence we choose the shift first. If we do, then, in the remaining days of the week, how do we prioritize so that we bring in all that is important to us?

Getting the right job, for the right amount of money sounds like the perfect recipe. But if having to work extra for that extra bit of money that infringes on your family time then that needs to be taken into consideration and modification is vital.

If money overtakes our priority then our state of mind suffers more than our body. We undergo guilt feelings of neglect and helplessness. Before we know it, it can lead to depression and behaviour changes.

## *Points to Consider*

If we see certain inappropriate behaviour changes in our colleagues or in their state of mind, it is important to approach them if you can or ask an appropriate person to do so. There is many help available in every hospital for those requiring help in financial situations.

## *Savings for the future*

Many staff come from different countries. Some have great responsibilities back home to their family. It is important to look into ways to save for your family.

Lack of savings can lead to anxiety and lack of focus on your work. There are many opportunities available from various resources at your work, various banks or the RCN (Royal College of Nursing) that can help you plan for the future.

Take advantage of these resources. I know a few friends that still keep a Piggy Bank. One Piggy is for annual savings and one is for annual vacations. They seriously take an interest in putting coins away every day.

## *Does Charity Really Begin at Home?*

Most healthcare professionals enjoy giving to charity once they become qualified. We belong to a noble profession. Charity is a personal choice as you are offering your time or your money. Setting a budget helps you to not over give. Balance is important.

We tend to use our right hand to give and left hand to receive. Both hands need to be in a state of equilibrium. By giving too much we lose our balance. With no balance, we invite disease processes to take over our minds.

Be conscious of who we give to. If our family is too demanding and unsupportive perhaps it is a sign to draw limitations and rules as to what we want to give and how much. Consider what are we giving too much of. Is it our valuable time or our valuable money? As professionals, time is money. We spend a lot of our personal money on courses. Most courses and conferences are very expensive. Nevertheless, due to the nature of our work, we study to keep abreast of our education. Be conscious that your money is well spent.

When we volunteer to charities, it is important to analyse in totality the charity you working with and how they value your training and expertise. Most charities will accommodate you with food and accommodation.

But some charities will expect your expertise and money. So measure that with how much time and money you giving to your family and how much time or money you have to give to charity. If you don't measure it correctly, it can lead to frustration and imbalance in your energy and health.

## *Your Time is Money*

Time is a precious gift. Our time on earth is limited. Every second therefore needs to be time well spent. Sadly not many people value time. People value money instead. Being short staffed can be quite a challenge and a risk. Know that your time is your money. You are a professional.

It is important to ask your manager if you will be paid for extra time for the work completed. Or you may want to negotiate time back. Be conscious that all staff should get equal time back. It is about everybody. Self-consciousness is limiting; it allows opportunities for jealousy, anger, and hatred to develop.

This hinders wellbeing. Speaking up for colleagues and supporting each other creates an expansive and positive relationship. Respecting one's time and effort reveals how you respect your time and effort. That is how you will be respected. Here are a few deep questions that may help you get unstuck from money issues. Take time to think about and investigate from within about each question.

- Do you ask for payment for overtime work?

  _____

- What holds you back from asking for your time or extra pay?

  _____

- What channels of communication can you use at your workplace to discuss your concerns on this?

  _____

- What is your relationship with money?

  _____

- Do you have any limiting belief systems?

  _____

- Now make a list of your income and expenses
  for the month

  List your income        List your expenses

  _____     _____

  _____     _____

  _____     _____

  _____     _____

  _____     _____

  Total                   Total

  Do you see your expense higher than your
  income? If yes.

  _____

  What can you exclude or do about your high
  expense

  _____

## *Reflective Questions*

What is the most valuable message you received in this chapter?

_____

What will you do different based on what you've learnt?

_____

How will you ensure you do what you've written above in previous question?

_____

_____

What's been your light bulb moment whilst reading this chapter?

_____

How much of your own stress comes from money issues?

_____

# Section C

# RELATIONSHIPS

*"To be kind is more important than to be right. Many times what people need is not a brilliant mind that speaks but a special heart that listens"*

—Unknown Author

# Chapter 3
# PROFESSIONAL ETIQUETTE

## *Words Have Power; Use Them Wisely!*

As healthcare professionals, our words carry power and authority. Therefore, we need to be conscious of how we speak. Every day we have to speak with patients, colleagues and relatives. If we speak well, be honest and speak with integrity it instils faith and trust in our patients and colleagues around us.

It's important to say what we mean and mean what we say. We should not be afraid to repeat our words or explain it differently if we are not understood. Words can make or break a person. It can have a huge impact on a person's mental health. It is of vital importance that we communicate correctly. Speak always from the heart. The words become heartfelt. It can trigger and offload a lot of emotional baggage from a person if the words are spoken from the heart. We should only ask a question if we require an answer. Never ask a question to trap someone or embarrass someone. It reveals your state of your consciousness. If you catch yourself in this situation, that is ok. Being aware is the first step to healing.

There is room for correction and improvement. Ask from a humble state of being. This will not only improve your mental health but will earn you a lot of respect. When you write, know that you will be judged on your writing. Negative and positive feedback can have an impact on your conscious wellbeing. When you write, write well.

Have your own stylish handwriting that represents you. On most hospitals now, we have computerised notes. Still you can pay attention to your grammar and style of writing. It's a good skill to have and will earn you a lot of respect. Patients notes are important documents. If you follow the hospital and local guidelines, then this will lesson any tension in your mental health, because you are less likely to have errors. There will be very little for someone to correct you on.

When you write, be consistent in your report writing. If you are focused, then you will be able to clearly write your reports without omitting important points.

## *The Law of Karma*

What you put out comes back to you tenfold is the old wise words that explain Karma. So be careful what you put out! It will come back in ways you least imagined. I literally mean that. "As you sow, so shall you reap". Always do things with good intention. The pain or pleasure we cause others will eventually return to us. Therefore,

Whatever pain or pleasure we are experiencing now is a result of our previous activities. For the goodness of our wellbeing, it is important for us to keep this in mind always.

If our activities are incorrect then our wellbeing suffers. If we find ourselves in situations like this, know that you can always apologise and ask for forgiveness so that we can move on. Forgiveness is very healing. Karma is observed by that invisible one whom we refer to as the Super-Soul. According to Vedic literature the super soul is the one who:

- knows everything, past present and future

- keeps track of our karmic accounts

- arranges for the particular body and circumstances we get in life

- makes sure we get the karmic reactions we deserve by both giving us knowledge, forgetfulness, remembrance and inspiration.

- awards the living beings what they desire and deserve

Our intention is always good and is only to serve our patients, visitors, and colleagues well. Therefore, when we go home at night and put our heads on the pillow we know we have done the best we can and will suffer no karmic reactions. Our intention should always be to keep a good relationship with our colleagues. Relationships are important; they define you.

Good relationships can provide tremendous impetus on your journey to conscious wellbeing. Only you have the power to make your relationships work. There is always a point where you can start again.

## *Am I Serving in the Right Capacity?*

It is important here to know and clearly understand our roles in our profession. Where do we fit in with our roles and exactly what our job description involves? This helps us form boundaries. Sometimes we see jealousy and competition for a post, mostly likely a senior post or the one that pays more. It is important to recognise your potential when applying for such a post.

## *Some questions to consider:*

- Do you have what it takes for that role advertised?

  _____

- Do you have the experience and expertise to fulfil your role?

  _____

- Is there a vacancy available for that role?

  _____

- If the answer is No.

  Then instead of you trying to find ways to get rid of the person already in that role which you fancy for yourself, perhaps it is time to consider exactly what is your role? Or as yourself, should you seek employment elsewhere?

  _____

## *Some other questions to consider:*

- Are you there to support the person?

- Are you able to help a person climb the professional ladder?

- Are you just meant to be the space to hold the energy for the person so that they can grow to be a better person in their profession.

- All the above points are a vital role we all play in life. We just have to play our role well.

If you know and understand your life purpose then this is easy. If you do not then this can be quite challenging. Not everyone has taken birth to be in charge. Not everyone wants to be in charge. Knowing and understanding your role within your department and being very clear in your mind and heart is very important otherwise this will create lot of anxiety within you and those around you. Be satisfied with your role.

## *Important questions to ask here:*

- **How do I treat others?**

- **How do others treat me?**

When I did my VIP and royal nursing course, I learned to respect people's space, their lifestyle and the manner in which they would like to be addressed. By answering these important questions, you will get to know more about yourself and what you putting out to the world. How you treat others will depend upon how you treat yourself.

## *Dealing with Hurt*

When we get hurt, who does the hurt belong to? The hurt belongs to us. Not the person who hurt us. This is such a vital feedback mechanism from our body that shows us what we need to work on our self now. So do not hate the haters.

Thank them for showing you the mirror. Not many people can be upfront and honest with you. Some are too afraid of your reaction. Some are too afraid what others may say or judge them. If we are fortunate enough then we may meet someone who is upfront and honest with us and tell us straightforwardly about us.

This mirror appears in front of us to tell us something about us. We need to be open to listen. We need to be clear that this is not a vindictive motive but an honest gesture for our highest good. Know when to let go. Learn about yourself quickly so that you are quick enough to help yourself. There are going to be colleagues who don't think before what they say.

## The "first story" manager:

There will be that manager who will take only the first story that comes to their office without investigating the whole story and they may say hurtful things to you because your story came second to their office. Some colleagues and bosses are never going to be possible to work with.

In times like this, your strength shows as to how you deal with the situation. These situations have choices. You either deal with it the best way you know and transcend it. Or you walk away and call it a day. Walking away does not mean you are weak and cannot deal with it. Some things are just not worth your energy to deal with or to deal with at that moment of time. These are the moments when people reveal themselves. You just need to learn people quickly without judgment and know how best to deal with it.

Do not let the hurt fester and grow deep roots into you. Pull out the weeds of hurt. Go to the core of the pain, feel the pain, and deal with that. Sometimes it is good to speak to a friend who knows you well and can help you shed some light into your hurt.

Sometimes the friend may highlight stuff you never thought about. When dealing with the hurt, think about and feel that hurt. Embrace the hurt. The more you embrace it the smaller it gets. The more you resist or fight it, the larger it expands. Cry if you need to.

Hurt always hurts! It is important to let it out. Know your friends or who you can talk to. Consider speaking to someone you can trust. Someone you know who will not break that trust and cause another hurt. Welcome sadness. Feel it. The more you embrace it the smaller sadness gets. If we react to stressful situations our blood ph changes to become more acidic.This leads to decreased blood flow to vital organs while our body is reacting to fight or flight responses.

We can increase inflammatory responses in our body if we do not deal with it. Your value does not suddenly decease based on someone else's inability to see your worth. Value your worth, and keep adding value to it. Move on swiftly! Grow socially and emotionally!

## *Wear Your Uniform Like a Nightingale*

I always say to my students, wear your uniform like a Nightingale. Your badges and your distinguishing devices are what you worked hard for. Wear them with humble pride for the most beautiful profession. When you dress well and look neat and tidy, that looks appealing to the eye. We living in a world where people are eye candy and like things that look nice. If you wear your uniform well, observe the respect that comes your way.

Keep your shoes nice, shiny, and clean. A perfectly groomed hospital staff is the pride of the hospital. Thank your feet every day for carrying you through the day. Get regular foot care and foot massage. Long hours of standing take a toll on your feet. Many places offer special discounts for hospital staff in gratitude for the work they do.

Find them and utilize their services. During Nurses week, if you cannot find a nice gift for your nursing friends then I recommend I foot massage voucher. It goes a long way. We belong to a beautiful profession called nursing where we earn respect.

If you reading this book and belong to another profession then know whatever profession you belong to, be proud of it from a humble state of being. You worked hard to belong and you deserve it. For professions with uniform, we are judged by our appearance no matter what. Good, refined grooming without being vain makes us automatically feel better. Paying special attention to short neatly cut nails, hair up above the collar and clean shoes.

This helps us to be more disciplined. When you pay attention to your personal grooming then watch your walk change. Walk tall, no slouching and head up high. It's important to adopt a good professional walk. Walking without slouching will help prevent backache and give you a good posture.

To keep a good posture, stand up against a wall with your back head and shoulders pressed against the wall. Breathe in and out slightly arching your back when you breathe out gently. Do this five times every day for a good posture. Find your own style and swag. Exude confidence especially when speaking to patients and relatives. Avoid slang and jargon. Study your subjects regularly. Keep on top of your CPD (Continuing Professional Development) and Competencies. Knowledge is power. Once you have knowledge and experience you can speak fluently on the subject. This will earn you a lot of respect.

Develop the right attitude when in uniform. Know you are part of a whole. The minute you entertain an attitude of "Us" and 'Them", Then you start a division. We are one NHS Trust OR one company and need to work together. Never moan about management or other departments.

That separates you from the whole. If colleagues around you happen to do that, which can sometimes happen then it is our duty to remind them and bring them back to the wholeness again.

Remind them that we are part of the same Trust.

## *Reflective Questions*

- What is the most valuable message you received in this chapter?

  _____

  _____

- What will you do different based on what you've learned?

  _____

  _____

- How will you ensure you do what you've written above in previous question?

  _____

  _____

- What's been your light bulb moment whilst reading this chapter?

  _____

  _____

# Section D

# ENVIRONMENT

*"The environment is where we all meet, where we all have a mutual interest, it is the one thing all of us share"*

—Lady Bird Johnson

# Chapter 4

# WORK ETHICS

## *What Is My Work Ethic?*

To be in a job, it is important to know the work ethics of the place. If we do not know the work ethics, it can have a negative impact on our health and wellbeing by us not practicing our codes of conduct.

What exactly then is work ethics? Work Ethics is the values of the industry we work in. Every Industry or department may have a different set of values. It will be in your best interest to learn about the values at your workplace on induction.

Each hospital has their own value system. For example, a value system could include the following five core values as part of their daily practice. They are Honesty, Equality, Accountability, Respect and Teamwork. If someone from the organisation feel that these values are not followed, it is their duty to discuss or express their feelings. It is advisable to learn more about the work culture before going for an interview as this will help you to decide whether you can fit into that team or not.

## *What Is My Work Environment Like?*

It is important to note that people don't leave jobs, they leave toxic work culture environments. People gracefully resign jobs for a more meaningful position. Toxic environments make people sick in their minds and their physical health. We lose our best colleagues in these sort of environment. It's a classic environment where projects fail. We work in an industry for wellness.

But it is important to understand what the signs are of a toxic environment so that you can detect it early and try to do something about it. So what are some of the signs of a toxic environment?

- Excessive control with heavy rules and regulations

- Disrespect in any form

- Belittlement

- Any form of harassment and bullying

- Ignoring. Pretending not to hear or listen. Walking past colleagues without greeting.

- Listening to selected colleagues only

- Unequal opportunities for all

- Constantly gagging complainers instead of listening

- Lack of compassion

- Managers & staff showing no interest in improving the environment

Working in an environment like this stunts our growth and feeds our soul with negativity. Instead of opening our pathways to a work journey well- travelled, we end up on a journey less- travelled especially if we do not have a mentor to support us to rise above the obstacles or help change the environment. Every one of us has a duty of care to create a positive and healthy working environment.

A conscious wellbeing environment can be encouraged in every workplace and developed into a toxic free culture. How can we bring that into our everyday life? Here is a list of a few simple things we can do.

- Listen with full attention when someone speaks without interrupting

- Involve all in what we do

- Be honest with each other

- Appreciate all

- Giving recognition to a job well done

- Support each other

- Have integrity

- Stay steady in Commitment and Dedication

- Empower people

- Value hard work

Your greatness lies not merely on what you achieve but what you give. Practicing compassion in your work life results in a balanced, dignified, successful work life. Bringing compassion to our work environment guarantees us a successful work environment.

Compassion is such a vital skill to possess for a successful work life yet hospitals never advertise a job for such a skill. Instead, we see adverts for clinical skills. It is taken for granted that everyone working in a healthcare environment possess compassionate skills.

Compassion allows us to align our human values with the way we treat others and the way we are treated at work. If we treat people well then they will feel satisfied and dignified at work. They will then in return treat others as they are treated at work. It is a domino effect. Some areas we can consider being more compassionate:

- Creating a blame free or confrontational free zone by assuming everyone has a good intention when things go wrong

- Decreasing constant tension for making people feel more comfortable in their work environment

- Creating a zone in which people don't feel like they are being paid to come and suffer at work

- Disadvantages of an un-compassionate work environment

- Employees suffer burn out

- Managers become fatigued

- clients/customers or patients can feel it in the quality of their experience

- Advantages of compassionate work environment

- loyalty in staff retention

- High quality customer care

- Better care to patients or clients

- Improved staff camaraderie

- Caring for each other improves

Most work places do not support or teach humility and failure. As a result, we resort to a blame culture.

By blaming others, we get an opportunity to be recognised and earn brownie points. We fail to practice self-compassion. When we practice self-compassion we open ourself out to being self-accountable, we allow ourselves self-reflection and we accept our own imperfections.

In a world fixated by perfection and recognition, being vulnerable can lead to feelings of guilt, shame and embarrassment. Compassion starts with a simple choice to put yourself in the shoes of others, feel what they feeling and acknowledge that people do not come to work deliberately to be difficult. It is possible that someone is having a bad personal experience or an accumulation of unresolved issues. Unless we do not investigate, we will never know what that person is going through.

At work, it is important for us to unite and get to know our colleagues and their truths so that we can better shower them with a more compassionate outcome. Know that your colleagues always have good intentions. Get to know the whole truth before judging anyone.

## *Comparison*

If you work in an environment where people keep comparing themselves with you or each other, this environment hinders connection or a sense of coming together. If we keep comparing then we cannot connect. Comparing dispels connection. Have you ever been in a situation where you trying to explain to someone your situation and instead of them attentively listening they are thinking of their situation within your story?

When you have completed your explanation then instead of acknowledging what you said they immediately start responding of what it feels like for them. These are people you want to distance yourself from if you are unable to resolve to a connection. They will forever compare themselves to you.

## *Beliefs*

Beliefs affect our wellbeing. Beliefs exist because we do not investigate it. We just believe. We trust the source blindly. Sadly, many people run their life on a "belief culture".

They fail to investigate the facts. Or they too scared to change their belief if their work teams function on a gang mentality. They do not want to be singled out. Mahatma Gandhi said:

- Your beliefs become your thoughts,

- Your words become your actions,

- Your actions become your habits,

- Your habits become your values,

- Your values become your destiny

## *Friend or Foe*

Who are the ones that pick you up at work? It is important to be conscious of who are the ones that hold your hand and show you the way or the ones that have your back. These are the people you want to be around. They bring out the best in you and have a stake in you.

This will help you bring out more miraculous things in you. Even talents you never knew you had. These are the ladders in your life. They allow you to step on them so that you can go to the next level. They expect nothing in return. They are humble compassionate, dedicated souls. Success is not a destination. It is a journey.

Most of us have forgotten that we are all capable of being successful. I always believe that when you reach the top of the ladder then it is your duty to lend a hand down to pick the next person up. This is what makes our professional journey so magical. Find those hands and lean on it. Avoid those that keep their hands to themselves. It is not the journey you want to take.

As the famous saying goes, "People were created to be loved, not compared. Things were created to be used, not competed against. The reason why we have so much chaos in our head and around us is because people are used and things are loved." Some questions we need to ask ourselves.

Do people around me like me irrespective of anything or they like what I have either ideas, position or material stuff. The ones who will like you irrespectively are the ones you want in your life. Never gossip! People who are idle gossip. Our workplace is too busy to get involved with gossip. If you find yourself gossiping then know your mind is becoming idle, you do not have enough work on your hands and you need to do something about it.

We living in a world of fake news. If you hear a story or gossip, it important that you find the bottom of the story and not just trust the person relaying the information to you. It's your duty to respect everyone and give everyone a fair opportunity. Failure to do so is a lack of responsibility on your part.

Gossiping and spreading fake news about our colleagues is not a professional attitude to adopt. Find a way to evade such situations. The golden rule is "If you hear anything, do not pass it on".

When we place upon our friendships with neglect, abuse and thoughtless action then we shut ourselves off from the support that makes

life easier to bear. Our support system shuts
down. We not conditioned to be our true self.
Many people find it hard, to be their true self. It is
something we learn along the way. As humans,
we always learning. Be open to learning and
willing to change.

## Who Supports Your Work?

Emotion should never be a slave to customs.
Each colleague needs to be seen as a whole.
Whatever they can deliver and whatever their
weaknesses are in the team. Only focusing on
the negatives without considering the effort,
quality of work and time colleagues devote to
their work will only enslave you.

We don't value good quality support staff in
the name of custom and regulation. Sometimes
staff forget, that whatever shifts the bank
nurse is working, that that is his or her salary.
They choose to do bank so that they can have
flexibility of hours. They may be supporting
charities and volunteer their time in community
work thereby choosing to be on the bank staff.
But have we bothered to find out their journey?
Permanent staff already have a month end

salary. We do not think out of the box. We do not think how that bank nurse will pay her bills. Support staff do not work 52 weeks in a year.

How will she/he take care of herself? Lack of support to bank staff who save our hospitals a lot of agency shifts can lead to a loss of some very high quality nurses who humbly resign from their opportunity to earn a lot of money through agency and settle for a much smaller amount of money on the bank.

Instead of saluting their sacrifice, we cancel their shifts. We don't fully support their work and sometimes some people view them as they are not "our staff" because they not permanently based. We see them as aliens. Yet we all employed by the same employers. But when we short of staff then we begging for their service.

This kind of behaviour reveals the quality of your heart chakra. Cleansing your heart chakra will help you to have more compassion for your colleagues, respect all staff equally, and make the right decisions.

There are still many nurses who respect the bank staff and honour their support at times of needs especially now that we having a shortage of nurses worldwide. Many managers sincerely support bank staff and appreciate their loyalty because they know when its staff shortage then we really depend on our bank staff. Whatever you do, you do for the best interest of the patient.

If your colleagues criticise your work, consider from what place this complaint is coming from before you react. If it is from a place to help you grow and improve yourself then these ones that support your work no matter how negative the comments might be. Consider who is making the complaints. Is it someone who has never shown any personal growth? Is it someone who is a consistent complainer? The complaint needs to be legitimate and serve the right purpose for a positive outcome. It should never be for a personal endeavour or a gang mentality that wishes to hinder your progress. When someone else's failure feels like victory to us, then we are the greatest failures in this world.

Consider what you do when you see someone failing. Do you only support them if they are from your country, community, culture or team? If we selectively support persons, then it is not only the other person who is failing, it is us who is failing too. Supporting each other and carrying each other when we fall is the greatest gift you can give to your colleagues. It is your duty to support each other.

If we find unsupportive people on our work journey, then it is important to acknowledge who they are. In our minds and heart, we can thank them for crossing our paths and giving us the opportunity to know what we do not want in our lives. Psychically you can wish them well and keep a professional distance. Jay Shetty says, "If you do not heal the hurt of your past, you will bleed the whole of your future".

**Points**: List the people who support you. Next to it, list how they support you. How do you show gratitude for your support?

Do you say thank you or remember their birthdays or give them a gift on nurses day?

## *Family and Loved Ones*

Family and loved ones are our greatest support in working life. They are our pillars. We cannot thank them enough. In London, the majority of the staff are foreigners and have family and friends in another country. It is of vital importance to keep in touch with our family and friends. Take time out to call them, spend quality time. With technology nowadays, it is very easy to stay in touch. Its more about how we manage that time to stay in touch. If we set aside quality time, there will be no space in your life to deal with regret, guilt and forgiveness. If you go on holidays regularly, call each other regularly; meet as often as you can then you achieving the best quality relationship possible. Time passes us by so quickly. If we fail to share our lives with our loved ones then we suffer consequences in our minds.

The more time, effort and energy we put into our relationships, the more will come back to us. We exchange loving relationships with each other. Be around people you love. Be generous with your time with them. When we meet, we lift each other's spirits.

We exchange loving energy when we meet loved ones. We learn to experience how to love from each other. It's a good opportunity to learn to how to receive. At work we always in a state of giving, but in a loving relationship we give and we receiving naturally without expecting anything in return.

## *Can Colleagues Be Friends?*

Firstly, we have to understand what our understanding of a friend is and what is involved in a friendship. Then we need to understand what does colleagues mean and what a professional work relationship is.

When we clear about this then our path to conscious wellbeing on duty is healthy. Friends are people who love you and support you without expecting anything in return. Certainly, colleagues can be friends.

Placing boundaries and knowing the professional distance is important to bear in mind when you working together with friends. It is important not to take anything for granted in the name of friendship. In isolated cases, we see when two friends are working together, then one will be in charge and one will be the floater not allocated to any specific job description.

Such behaviour can disturb the team. It can come across as unfair. If we are fully focused, understand our roles, achieve our goals, be fully conscious of exactly what is our duty then such behaviour will not survive in the work place. This results in a positive outcome. To create good relationships in the work place two guidelines are vital. Communication and Cooperation; communication helps us to establish a link with the other person.

Cooperation helps us to be more productive. Relationships should always have equal benefits that each person is getting equal opportunities out of the relationship.

## *Setting Personal Standards*

Setting personal standards is a key to self respect. It is important to know yourself and what you will and will not do. If you do not have personal standards you will find yourself following others standards and you can easily lose yourself and your core values.

Know when you will not cross that line and stick to it. Understand our codes of conduct and use that to help you in personal standard setting. You can never go wrong. But other basic personal settings to consider are your interaction like are you prepared to work weekends, or nights, or will you play by the rules at all times or will you have a moral code which you will not break no matter what.

Take time out and think about what you want to achieve and how you would like to be remembered after you leave the industry. That will help you set a good standard. Write it down and refer to it every now and again or during appraisal times to keep a check on how you doing. Know when you can stay late at work or go early.

### Keep your standards.

If you take advantage of situations then you suffer the consequence of guilt. Going of early most times without permission or deserving it is like stealing work time. It's a theft. There are consequences to it. Stick to your standards and save the guilt. Everybody has a bad day at work. Set your standards as to how you intend to deal with those days. Things to consider here is your relationship to food, drugs, sleep and mood.

Set your standards on how you going to deal with a bad day at work. When you are happy and healthy on the inside, your relationships thrive. Everything around you is harmonious. Meditation is the perfect path for deep connection, fulfilled life and harmonious relationship with yourself and all things around you.

## *Dealing with Negativity at Work*

There will always be someone who does not like you or what you do. Have faith in yourself. Believe in your work. People may say many things but it may not necessarily be the truth. Opinions are welcome.

But opinions are only a part of the whole truth, to know the truth you need to know the whole information and in the context it is coming from. You need to know who is giving you the opinion and what reliability factor they possess. Hearing good news about a person can affect people differently.

How it affects us acts as a barometer of how emotionally healthy we are. Just as pain serves, as a barometer that something is wrong, like that negative emotions serves as an indicator as to what we need to work on. Some relationships can be toxic. Sometimes we have to walk away from it. However, at work it is important to keep a professional distance. Do not cut people out of your life. Rather limit your interaction with them. You never know when you going to need them. People can change.

Life's experience changes people if they willing to learn. People that change work on themselves. Therefore, we need to applaud people who make an effort to change themselves for their highest good.

Everybody deserves a chance, a hand in help and Time. We are a caring Industry so we owe it to ourselves. Dealing with negativity at work can be quite challenging and also quite exciting to watch when things can be turned around. Never take sides.

It leads to further negativity. Try to see both sides of the story without ignoring both parties. This comes from a lot of practice and experience how you handle negativity. Knowing what words to use appropriately and how to change mindsets. We all make mistakes and said the wrong things in the past. But it is how we unlearn and put into practice the new learning. In a negative situation, it is important to always stay calm and be diplomatic.

Know when to keep your opinions to yourself. Only express yourself if someone requests you. You don't have to give an opinion for everything. There is no need to always be in conversation.

If you find yourself in this situation then it is time to ask yourself, why do you like to be heard? Or why do you like the sound of your voice so much? Think about it. Reflect on it. Reflect on why your opinion is so important at every conversation.

Avoid getting personal on duty and criticising the culture of the place as if you are different from it. We are responsible for the negativity we create around us if we don't deal with it appropriately. I know someone who constantly squeals saying they don't know how to do off duties, they don't know how to handover, they don't know how to allocate staff. All this "THEY" separates the complainer from the complaint and they think they are separate from both. But did the complainer make an effort to address the issues.

Perhaps more training is needed in the department for delegation skills, more education or relocating job roles. Reporting through the proper channels of communication will help alleviate negativity in the work place. If the complaint has not been followed up, then it can be escalated to a higher authority in a very professional way. Make sure you write everything down. Keep records of date, Time and persons reported to.

There is only one message for moaners that they should try to enjoy what is going on around them or leave. One cannot be happy with consistent moaning. The old saying goes, if you content at home then there is nothing you need to prove at work. Finding the contentment in your inner being is the key. Next time you catch yourself frequently moaning then consider what is lacking in your personal life. Not everyone will agree with you. Everyone is on their own journey and may have their own lessons to learn. People will agree with you based on their level of consciousness and exposure to that subject. It is important here to know we are here to deliver the best possible care to our patients from our highest good.

Nursing is one of the profession that allows us to practice being humble. This is purely due to the way we work. Today we may take charge of a shift. That puts us in a position of authority. The nest day someone else is in charge then this puts us in a position to follow and support the authority for that day.

By practicing this wholeheartedly allows us to put into practice our humbleness. We are very fortunate that our profession can give us wonderful humanistic qualities to improve. In central London, we have nurses from several different countries. Many still have a problem with detachment from their country and this is seen in their ability to socialise only with their country folks. You can sometimes only get them interested if their compatriot is part of it. That is how attached some people are. Sometimes, they go as far as only employing someone who is from their country.

There is a big difference between being patriotic and attachment. Attachment is a disease. Sometimes, people do not know they are suffering from attachment. Attachment does not help to unite a workforce.

Understanding that you are a global citizen and that everyone is important opens our eyes to accept everyone and bring in new talents we otherwise would not be able to experience if we just worked with our own fellow citizens in a foreign location.

If we open to all then we open to learning new ways of working and developing ourselves. It is ok if not everyone agrees with you. It is also ok if you the only one who agrees with yourself. Everyone has a right to his or her own opinion.

When we delegate staff or allocate staff, know that everyone has their opinion and how you should have done it. Make your own decision and stick with it. Believe in yourself that this is the right decision at this moment.

Sometimes, it's hard to delegate friends and staff you worked with for a long time. As the saying goes, "If it feels scary and painful then that's real delegation". Whatever you do, you do for the best interest of the patient or client.

## *Mentorship and Peer Appraisal*

Everyone needs a mentor. Mentors are valuable gifts at work. We seldom acknowledge that. We all need to learn from someone who already knows better than us. It makes our journey easier and quicker. It is only until recent years that student nurses and doctors lived at home. Many lived in a nurse's home and left home quite young to start their career.

They had very little parental support on a daily basis and relied heavily on nurse mentors and senior staff for personal growth. Hence, we are ever forgiving to our very senior colleagues who have given up their comforts at a tender age to join our profession many years ago.

## *Peer Appraisal*

Peers are people on the same level as us. They can see things as we do. Being appraised by a peer is a gift. It opens up a different level of accepting our strengths and weaknesses.

Positive and constructive feedback is what we want at work to give us a meaningful journey through work. Words have power to change us. Peers have the power to bring out the best in us. As peers, it is our responsibility to correct and add value to someone's work journey.

## *Mentors*

Mentors can be great leaders and guide the pathway of their team members in the right direction. We always believed leaders needed eloquence and charisma but in conscious wellbeing, three core mental qualities are vital:

- mindfulness,
- selflessness and
- compassion.

With these three ways, one can better engage their teams and meet challenges in our rapidly growing environment. You cannot manage other people if you do not know how to manage yourself first.

When the mentor can understand his mind, personality and values then only can he lead effectively. In our jobs, we are accustomed to giving senior positions to those with a deserving merit certificate. Managers should have in mind when choosing positions for senior staff if the person they chose have the ability to be a mentor to others apart from their clinical expertise.

There are mentors in name only who do not actually do any mentoring and treat the appraisal as a paper exercise so that all the boxes can be ticked. This is such a waste of resources and an opportunity to build someone's career. In this way, leadership starts in the mind. If we take care of our staff, they will take care of the patients and guests and the work will take care of itself.

## *Appraisal*

We all seek feedback from our peers, managers and clients. It is very important for us to get feedback and be open minded about it. Getting feedback from those above you , your level and below you is a good 360 degree appraisal. This feedback helps us understand our mental and social health and wellbeing.

It is an opportunity to get to know our strengths, weaknesses, things we need to focus on, things we need to work less on to reserve our energy for something better. Honest feedback must be appreciated. This kind of feedback is our building block. If problems are not identified early enough, then we could go on making the same mistake without knowing.

It is important to appreciate and be grateful for receiving feedback. Appraisals help us to know what is expected of us and if we reaching that expectancy. Hearing good news about other people can affect some. Not everyone has had a very successful life, so they are not accustomed to good news.

## *Reflective Questions*

What is the most valuable message you received in this chapter?

_____

_____


What will you do different based on what you've learnt?

_____

_____


How will you ensure you do what you've written above in previous question?

_____

_____


What's been your light bulb moment whilst reading so far?

_____

_____

Is your workplace toxic? If yes, what will you do about it?

_____

_____

How compassionate are your colleagues?

_____

_____

How compassionate are you to others?

_____

_____

# Section E

# HEALTH

*"It is health that is real wealth and not pieces of gold and silver"*

—Mahatma Gandhi

# Chapter 5
## ME TIME

### *Conscious Yoga*

It is important to listen to the rhythm of your body. Your rhythm will tell you how you are doing. Finding that me time is not a priority, it is a necessity. Yoga helps one to reach this space at a deep level. Yoga is not exercise.

It is a union with yourself. In addition, when you practice Mindfulness Yoga you become more in control of yourself, your body and your mind. You become empowered. Nobody can rock your boat so to speak. You become so aware of yourself and all that around you. Animals teach us many things.

Have you watched what a cat does the moment it wakes up from a sleep? It stretches its body. The cat has taught us how important it is to stretch your body before you get out of bed. Always remember, you don't exercise for yourself, you do the exercise to yourself. Sometimes we not sure which exercises are good for us. From my studies in Ayurveda I learnt that Mindfulness Yoga is good for the body as a whole. It is good for the body, mind and spirit. Mindfulness yoga is gentle and slow.

It involves flexing, stretching, breathing and lots of meditation throughout the class. From my yoga teacher, I learned that the surya namaskaran is one of the best exercises for healthcare providers.

It involves breathing & stretching techniques. It helps to strengthen the core and back muscles. Many nurses and doctors suffer backache.

## *Why is it important to strengthen your back muscle?*

Due to our poor activity, lack of exercise and poor posture we lose the strength of our back. Our back is not only important for keep the spine supported and healthy but it is important for the health of the entire body. Studying anatomy and physiology taught us that by strengthening the gluteus muscle we strengthen the mind.

## *Why is it important to strengthen your core?*

If we work in very busy units, we can sometimes feel very tired and believe that we have probably done enough exercise for the day so there is no need for doing more exercises as we may have exceeded our number of steps for the day.

This is a misconception. There are three elements involved in exercise: stretching, moving, and breathing. When all three are in action, we call it appropriate exercise that is required for wellbeing.

## *Meditation*

Meditation is nothing but spending quality time with your thoughts. Allowing them to form, then analysing and interpreting them without judgment. In order for us to meditate, we have to empty our minds of thoughts and allow them to pass through naturally.

You can do this with various resources like audio video tips, attend meditation classes or through a meditation coach. Our general experience of our life is governed by our thoughts. Meditation helps us shift from thinking (head) to feeling (heart).

It is a journey from the complexity of the mind to the simplicity of the heart. Meditation is an experience that comes to us naturally. We just have to give it space and time and be open to it.

Many people have a space in their home this is their sacred space. Whether they religious or an atheist. Whatever it is, know that this place you have created is your safe sacred space for you to take a journey within yourself. Before you leave home for work take time out for quiet time and meditation. Just 5-10 minutes of meditation every day at the same time, helps calm the nerves of the body and resets the body rhythm for the day. In your quiet time,

Ask yourself how do you feel today?

Listen and feel the response from your mind. Ask yourself how does your body feel right now. Feel the response from your body. Every day will be different. Observe what is the body reacting too. Be conscious of what works for you. Everybody has a different body type. So it's important for you to go along with your body needs.

## *Mantra Meditation*

Many colleagues will tell you how when they started mantra meditation that it changed their lives. Meditation and quiet time may not be for everyone. So you need to choose what path is best for you. Let us understand a little on meditation and mantra meditation.

**Man means mind.**

A mantra is a repetition of words with meaningful vibration that penetrate deep into your unconsciousness mind and realigns the vibration of your being. If you understand the meaning of the mantra, then it makes the practice more effective. Mantras have the ability to change the molecular structure in your cells.

That is why people feel renewed or rejuvenated after a mantra meditation session. Mantras can be chanted aloud, listened to or chanted mentally. Usually people who are seeking to learn meditation are people who want a more meaningful life. The greatest thing about meditation is it meets you exactly where you are and ushers you to where you want to go.

You will slowly see how bad habits change and you are guided in all the right direction. The Chopra Centre research has revealed that 8 weeks of regular practice has proven to show results.

## *Pranayama*

Prana is life force. Without a breath, we cannot stay alive. Therefore, it is of vital importance to all of us to learn how to breathe properly. Something that we normally do but never stop to think about. As healthcare professionals,

We are totally dependent on our brain. It takes about 7 years to be a fully experienced qualified Intensive Care Nurse or a qualified doctor.

It is important to note here how to oxygenate our brain so that it can better serve us. Pranayama is a breathing technique. If practiced correctly it provides oxygen to left and right side of the brain. It removes toxic gases we breathe in at work.

Many of us are exposed to inhalers, nebulisers and various gases in our work place. This technique helps to refresh the air in our brain and breathe out unwanted gases and thoughts.

## *Conscious Travel*

Take time out to travel, rejuvenate and reflect. Travel is the best investment you can make for yourself. Travel is an experience. People can take many things away from you but they cannot take away your experience.

Through your travel experience, you can receive a wealth of knowledge not available in any classroom. You do not have to be religious to go on pilgrimage. You can visit pilgrimage sites even if you spiritual. Pilgrimage sites are high energetic vortexes. Going on pilgrimage increases your energy levels. Some pilgrimage sites even have the ability to purify the energetic fields around you.

This is the reason why sometimes people can come back from a pilgrimage totally transformed. They become so relaxed and open to receive the energy from that place. Be wise to travel with the right guide to give yourself the best experience that will remain with you for a lifetime.

Walk for wellbeing on your travels. Use the malls as a shopping exercise. Keep a step count on your travels. Set yourself goals on every travel to improve your step count. Be aware of your surroundings, the colours, the smells, the tastes and noises. On my pilgrimage travels , amongst many things , one of the things I learnt from visiting Fatima in Portugal was the importance of going through a struggle. The more I tolerated, the stronger I became. This teaching helped me to practice tolerance on duty.

On my pilgrimage travels to Mayapur in India-Kolkata, I learnt love of God. I am not a religious person but rather spiritual. It also taught me that every step I take in that place cuts my karma. Who wants bad Karma?

So it is good to know that I can go somewhere to get rid of my bad karma and have the opportunity to start life fresh again. Everyone deserves a second chance. Before you book your holiday, listen to your body to understand what your body needs the most.

Depending on your body's needs, visiting places that are uplifting are places like crop circles parks and gardens, whilst Mountain areas are very good for grounding. Seaside can be very calming.

This helps to replenish your body's needs. You will know when you have accomplished your needs by the way you handle issues differently or by the your energy level. Sometimes one can go on holiday and return with a need for another holiday to recover.

Choice of travel according to your body and mind needs, are important. If you wish to know more of my Conscious Wellbeing Tours, then see my Facebook and twitter pages.

## *Listen Consciously to Your Body*

As healthcare professionals, we are good at looking after others but not always good at looking after ourselves. We all are guilty of that. It is important to listen to your body and understand the signals it is sending us.

These signals will help us to heal our bodies. In order to understand these signals, it is important to know what they mean and where the root cause lies. Through my years of experience as a nurse and nurse manager, I have observed that as healthcare professionals we suffer pain in 3 most common parts of our body, back, knee and stiff neck.

Pain is a good barometer to inform us about ourselves.

## *Back pain*

On a psychic level, our back represents something that "supports us". As the saying goes "I have your back". When we know someone has our back, we are reassured that we have support in life and in our work.

When realisation sets in and when you can feel and accept the support coming through, you immediately can experience the ease on your back pain. If you observe the departments that have a high rate of staff suffering from back ache. When you speak to the staff there, you will hear of how unsupported they are. When the issue is resolved and the staff regain support, then you can see how the backache reduces and staff resume work. Support yourself, ask for help, and gain confidence through knowledge and expertise. This will give you inner strength.

## *Knee Pain*

The knee is the area of pride and ego. When we become inflexible and wont bend and go with the flow then this area becomes restricted.

Becoming more understanding and compassionate releases the tension in this area.

## *Stiff neck*

The neck area is the area that represents flexibility. When this area regularly becomes stiff and painful then you should look into your stubborn inability to be flexibility.

Is it perhaps we failing to see the other sides of a story. It is important to see all sides of a situation.

## *Reflective Questions*

What is the most valuable message you received in this chapter?

_____

_____

What will you do different based on what you've learnt?

_____

_____

How will you ensure you do what you've written above in previous question?

_____

_____

What's been your light bulb moment whilst reading this chapter?

_____

_____

# Chapter 6

# A CONSCIOUS DIET

## Conscious Eating

Conscious eating means to be fully conscious of what you eating and basing what you eat, according to your body's needs. Eating consciously re-calibrates the mind. It stops binge eating. It helps change bad eating habits. Conscious eating is vital in maintaining a balanced diet.

The science of eating:

- Eat slowly do not rush

- Smell the food

- Taste the food is it sweet, bitter, sour?

- Feel the texture of the food in your mouth

- chew your food properly then swallow to aid a good digestion.

- Try not to talk and eat at the same time

Ayurveda has taught us to savour our food tasting each element of it. When we practice eating mindfully like this we become more aware of the tastes and texture on our tongue.

Be conscious of what you put into your mouth and what it is going to do to your body and mind. Food has an effect on both our body and mind. Be conscious of the colour of food you eat.

Too much red food or red meat can aggravate your mind. Green leafy vegetables are not only healthy but also calming to your mind. To be a vegetarian or vegan is a conscious choice you make for the wellbeing of your body mind and soul.

Anything that can be planted and shows signs of sprouting has life and consciousness.

That means plants also have consciousness. This is the reason why in some cultures the food is offered to God/ or power above before eating to not imbibe the karmic reaction of killing the plant. When we are young, we are taught to respect food. We are taught not place food on the floor, not to to trample on food and not to throw food.

Through Ayurveda we have learnt that food has consciousness hence we should respect food. Vegetarian foods should always be eaten fresh or cooked and eaten immediately. Eat only when you are hungry.

## *Food as Medicine*

Food is medicine. However, many accept food as an enjoyment for pleasurable satisfaction. This is when food becomes poison.

In this mood, we tend to satisfy our eyes and our tongues needs. We must not be mistaken; food can be an enjoyable experience but we should eat according to our body's needs. If we follow this mood, then there is no reason to diet. In the Ayurvedic section, we will learn how our body type differs. We need to eat foods according to our body types in order to maintain a balance and avoid disease processes.

Plant based foods increase your immunity and protect the body thereby healing to maintain wellness. You just have to look at the state of your tongue to know the health of your body. Ayurveda has taught us how to diagnose various body illness through the tongue. These diagnoses can be done through an ayurvedic doctor.

## *Shopping for Groceries*

Once you know your body type and what foods help keep you in the balance then grocery shopping can be a very satisfying experience knowing you shopping for your bodies needs. You taking responsibility for yourself.

Use your shopping time as a means for walking and as chance to increase your daily step-count.

Enjoy your shopping experience. Browse through the shelves and read the labels before purchasing. Avoid purchasing vegetables to be ripened at home. These items are sprayed with many chemicals for long shelf life.

It is advisable to purchase foods that are locally or homegrown. Organic foods are encouraged.

## *Water*

Your body is naturally intelligent. It will remind you when you are thirsty. Drink good quality water when you are thirsty. Water is very grounding! If you ever feel airy fairy, drink a lot of water and it will ground you. Water makes all the organs work nicely. A glass of lukewarm water is advisable as the first glass you have every morning.

Throughout the day, you can add fresh ginger and fresh mint leaves, which not only aids digestion but also helps to take away the boredom of drinking plain water.

Water reduces tiredness. If ever you feel tired, drink a glass of water. Watch thereafter how energising it is. If you work in warm areas or doing long hours in the scorching summer, try to drink more water to rehydrate.

If you someone who works with energy or practices energy medicine then the best water to drink is that which comes from volcanic areas. Water from this area is highly magnetic and high in energetic levels.

After a shift it is important to drink water to rid the body of any organisms that has been inhaled or entered through your skin on your shift. Never keep your bottle water near a computer or microwave. Water absorbs energy. So if it is kept in an area of high energy then it will absorb that energy.

If you know a Reiki master, request them to energise your water. It will uplift your mood. Drinking water immersed in crystals that best suit the intention you wish to achieve is very comforting. Crystals carry various different energies and intentions. Water immersed or placed around Rose Quartz crystals invites love into your heart and attracts loving relationships around you. This could be good to enhance team building.

## *Karma Free Milk (Ahimsa Milk)*

Karma free milk might sound like a new age milk. But it is a practice that has been going on for over 5000 years. It is described in the holy Vedas that milk taken from cows against their will is poisonous. What to speak of milk that is taken from who have had their calves forcibly taken away, who are kept in confined spaces and who are artificially inseminated.

In some cases, cows are tortured over a period of years and milk is forcibly removed to provide a whole community. Many researchers have shown us what happens to our blood when we and animals are tortured.

From these, we have seen how the chemistry of the blood changes to become more acidic with high levels of hormones excreted for survival; in essence, the pH of our blood changes.

Once we understand this, it is important to research which dairy does your milk come from. Enquire how the cows are cared for before you purchase the milk. As this can have a negative impact on your health and wellbeing.

There are many dairy farms that are dong highly quality dairy farming. Some will even invite you to come visit their farms. It is just a matter of being mindful of what you want to put into your body and what effects it will have on your body.

## Ayurveda

I spent many years in Kerala studying Ayurveda. Being a nurse, I was very interested scientific medicine, trying to understand how the body functions through natural therapies as well as western medicine. I have witnessed that in acute cases western medication and surgery works effectively. But for chronic cases mind-body therapies are more effective. Let us now try to understand a little of what is ayurveda.

## What is Ayurveda?

Ayurveda is a traditional healing system based on the laws of nature that dates back to over 5000 years. Ayur means life. Veda means science. So it's the science of life using the holistic approach. The mind and body are treated together and not separately. Balance = Body + Mind + Environment. To keep our body in balance we perform regular Ayurvedic detox. In this process, toxins are released from the body and nourishing food is offered to the body.

## *Mind*

We use the mind to pay attention to any imbalance in the body. If we are not in the right frame of mind or we are not conscious of our body through our mind then we may miss the clues our body gives us to signal ill health. We train our mind through the process of meditation.

## *Body*

All imbalances either emotional or scientific are revealed through our bodies. So we have to be observant what is normal or abnormal reaction for us in order to bring us back to the state of normality in which we can best function. All of us have different body types so will require different needs. Through western medicine, we can heal our body through surgery or medicine but our mind may not necessarily be healed. Hence, diseases in our body can recur.

## *Environment*

If our environment is not conducive to our wellbeing then we can suffer imbalance. Toxic words, thoughts, relationships and food can all add to a toxic environment. We are surrounded everyday by this toxicity and add to our life's struggles. Knowledge allows us to navigate our way through life's struggles.

**Some ayurvedic terminology :**

- Ama - toxic residue ( this can be visible on our tongue)

- Agni - digestive fire

- Ojas - healthy energy , healthy thoughts

If the Agni is good then we extract healthy Ojas, which leads to healthy wellbeing.

## *Ayurvedic Body types*

According to ayurveda our body type is classified into 3 types. Pitta, Vata, Kapha. Some of us can have a combination of these 3. Each body type has a combination of 2 elements. The Elements are Space, Air, Fire, Water, and Earth. It is best advice to get your body type diagnosed by an Ayurvedic practitioner. To help you simply understand the types I have briefly explained their characteristics. I hope you find it helpful.

- Vata is made up of Space and Air elements

- Pita is made up of Fire and Water elements

- Kapha is made up of Water and Earth elements

## *Vata*

Those of vata body types are usually filled with high energy. Their movements and thoughts are fast like the wind. They find it hard to sit still. They have many goals but not always complete it. Their body is usually lean and light.

## *Pita*

Those of pita body types are usually fiery, intense and rather serious people. Very focused people that are goal orientated. They are usually decision makers that make things happen. They have a strong digestion. Their build is usually medium muscular.

## *Kapha*

Those of kapha body type are usually calm and content. They quite happy to carry on with life and don't seem to like to add changes to their life. They very grounded in their mind. Physically they are heavy, sturdy and grounded. However they are usually happy with what is around them.

Once we understand the normal characteristics of these doshas then its easy to understand our body and mind when we get out of balance. This enables us to maintain a normal wellbeing. It helps us bring ourselves back to our normal state of being unique to us. We are human can go off balance due to many factors.

They key is to recognize that you out of balance or out of character as we say and knowing when and how to bring us back to balance. Ayurveda has taught us not to quickly judge people but to get to know their true self first.

Their imbalance may not necessary be their true self. When you can recognize this then you can be a great help and support to your colleagues when they out of balance or out of character as we say.

## *Dosha Imbalance*

### Imbalance of Vata

Due to the increased air elements, activity, as well as the excessive travelling, or over exposure to electronic equipment, and lack of sleep. Result in anxiety, restlessness, agitation, short temper, sensitive to stimuli, erratic thoughts; develop food sensitivities, cold peripheries.

### Imbalance of Pita

Due to the increased fire elements, eating excessive spicy foods, as well as increased workload, exposure to stress, exposure to extreme weather conditions. Result in a focused and rigid behaviour pattern, such as anger, being in a cranky mood, an inflammatory response on skin, my way or the highway attitude.

### Imbalance of Kapha

Due to increased earth and water elements, increase eating of heavy foods, decrease in bodily activity, sluggish digestion, excessive sleeping. Result in depression, slow thinking, weight gain, oedematous joints, don't care attitude, sweaty, TV potato couch kind of behaviour.

## *How to correct Dosha imbalance?*

### Vata

Eat warm comforting foods like soup, take warm baths, and establish routine sleep habits. Stay in company of Kapha dosha people. Wear or surround yourself with warm calming colors like brown, beige, white.

### Pita

Eat cooling foods, take cool bathes, spend time near seaside rivers or waterfalls, and walk in the park, all activity in moderation. Wear or surround yourself with soothing soft colours like blue, green.

### Kapha

Increase activity, routine exercises, and associate with vata body types. Avoid heavy foods like rice and potato. Wear or surround yourself with red and orange or any bright colours.

# *Conscious Wellbeing - Daily Detox (10 steps)*

Our body is intelligent and is able to detoxify all the time. Ayurveda has taught us that the body has nine houses and each house has its own complex and effective detox system to protect the body.

A daily Ayurvedic detox programme allows us to detox daily our body, mind and environment the natural way. Ayurveda is the most powerful caring system established over 5000 years ago by the great sages of India. The body's natural detox takes place before disease sets in. Stress, toxicity, eating unhealthy foods, increase in alcohol all result in increased cellular damage thereby increasing free radicals , increase premature aging and inflammatory response.

Awareness and daily detox protects our bodies from these extreme responses. There are many ways one can detox but here are a few simple methods you can use on a daily basis and if done correctly and daily will provide you with great results.

## *Sleep*

Sleep is a natural form of detox. We require a minimum of 7 hours of sleep daily. Whilst we sleep, the body uses a natural process of consolidating memory & thoughts and calming the mind. Whilst we sleep, hormones are naturally regulated. Cortisol levels are decreased. Our immune system normalises itself thereby improving our defence mechanisms. Breathing slows down and less oxygen consumption is utilised.

Sleep is the body's natural way of rejuvenating. There is many sleep therapy music and sleep Apps on the market to help one enter a deep relaxing sleep. Various bath soaks that contain lavender also helps one to unwind and ease into a relaxing sleepy mood. Do you want to get up every day in a healthy mood? Then opt for a deep 7-hour sleep.

## *The Tongue*

Ama (toxic residue) accumulates on the tongue whilst you sleep. You will find this coating on your tongue in the morning. Ama is also an accumulation of your unwanted thoughts and emotions. So instead of swallowing this back into your stomach, you can detox your tongue every morning with a tongue cleaner. There are many different varieties of tongue cleaners on the market. Use whatever is comfortable for you. As you scrape your tongue clean, notice daily the color and consistency of the Ama.

Notice how you feel as you become aware of your thoughts as you detox your thoughts. The tongue detox you can get started very quickly and detox yourself daily. It is an easy and inexpensive process.

## *Thoughts*

Positive thoughts give us peace of mind. A stream of good, positive thoughts decreases resentment. Good thoughts increase love and healthy relationships. Whatever thoughts we put out, return to us at the correct time. Be mindful of cursing and sending out negative thoughts as it will return when you least expect.

It's good to set a routine everyday day before you sleep to recap your day and observe what sort of thoughts come to your mind. Detox your thoughts daily to avoid a buildup of unwanted thoughts and unresolved issues. Observe your thoughts in general. As thoughts come and go, let it flow.

Observe what kind of thoughts come to you. Are they happy or sad thoughts? How does it make your body feel? Does it energise you or drains you. Don't be hard on yourself. As you meditate, you will learn how to bring yourself to your present moment. You will learn how to transcend negative thoughts through meditation.

## *Abhyanga (oil massage)*

This is an ayurvedic oil massage of the body with a dosha specific oil. The dosha specific oil is used to maintain the balance of your dosha and thereby maintaining wellbeing. The oil is usually pre mixed with herbs for the specific dosha. But if premixed oils are unavailable then specific base oils can be used. As we grow older and if we don't exercise then our lymphatic system slows down and becomes unable to rid the toxins in our bodies.

Lymphatic system does not have valves to push forward the waste material and relies on exercise and movement to push forward. Abhayanga is found to be very effective in aiding the movement of lymphatic drainage and removing toxic material.

A daily oil rub on your entire body in your morning and evening routine will provide many health benefits. Massage your body before a bath from the peripheries working towards the heart area is advised for an effective lymphatic drainage.

**Benefits:**

- Nourishment for the whole body

- Improved sleep patterns

- Good circulation and lymph drainage

- Musculoskeletal and nervous system health

- Healthy vision

- Good skin texture

- Oil for Vata dosha - Sesame oil

- Oil for Pita dosha - Coconut oil

- Oil for Kapha dosha- Almond oil

## *Incense*

Great monks and spiritual leaders know the calming effects of incense. Incense helps us to purify our senses. Certain specific incense aromas work specifically to soothe the nerves and bring a state of calm. This effect helps to relieve stress and tension in the muscle. Here are a few incense scents you can try to burn for wellbeing:

- Relaxing - Lavender

- Cleansing negative energies in your environment - Frankincense Sage

- Re-energising Citrus scented like lemon and orange

After a busy shift, try burning a lavender incense at home and feel the difference.

## *Bath Salts*

Working in environments of stress can be very harmful to the body as the body releases its toxins. Adding bath salts to your warm baths aids in drawing out impurities, toxins and pollutants through the skin. Salt has a positive ion effect and neutralises negative ions. When you experience a challenging day at work with a lot of negativity then try bathing in a tub of Pink bath salts and feel the difference. The pink salt will relax the body and soothe tired muscles. It will also remove toxins from the body and netralises negative ions.

## *Music Therapy*

Music has the ability to purify our hearing sense. Music is also a mood enhancer. Music can be used to enhance your wellbeing. Put on a music and observe what it does to your mind and the rhythm of your body.

Music has the ability to relax our senses or provide an upbeat mood if we are too relaxed. Hymns, chants and devotional music can soothe the mind as well as the heart.

Space cleansing music can also be used to clear your home and rid of negative energy. For this specified loud music is used. Loud devotional group singing accompanied by musical instruments can also help clear a space very quickly. A weekly space cleansing is advised.

South African africans have proved to us that by singing and creating a rhythm with your body you can walk long distances without being aware how long you have travelled. Many africans walk several kilometres in the villagers with the help of their own musical voice to keep the pace.

Music for therapy can be downloaded from various Music Apps.

## *Yoga*

Illustration: Suryanamaskar

Suryanamaskar is a sun salutation fitness programme in yoga. Science has taught us that suryanamaskaran is better than jogging and walking. The postures and movements in this workout involves a complete full body and mind workout. Thus, the experts advise yoga.

One round of surayanamaskar can take a minute to complete. Thus, 12 rounds can roughly be completed in 10 minutes. According to the Art of Living group, one round burns up to 13.90 calories for an average weighing person.

Many people believe yoga is a non-cardiac workout. Nevertheless, if suryanamsakaran is done at a fast pace, then it gives a complete cardiac workout and if done slowly it helps to relax the body.

Research has taught us that suryanamaskaran is one exercise that works directly on our glands (thyroid, pituitary, adrenals).

This practice has assured us if done correctly and regularly then we can achieve optimum metabolism, optimum levels of Vit D and effective working of all our glands. Yoga teachers have assured us that a daily practice of surynamaskar, which roughly takes 10 minutes, ensures an effective wellbeing workout. Benefits include:

- Strong back, good posture, strong body

- Radiant skin

- Hormonal balance

## *Nadhi Shodhana Pranayama*

Nadhi Shodhana Pranayama is alternate nostril breathing. it's a very vital breathing technique to learn for everyday practice. Oxygen is vital to our body. We cannot survive without oxygen.

Therefore,

Nadhi shodhana is very important for all of us to practice breathing properly for improving our oxygenation to all parts of our body thereby improving wellbeing. Before we even try to understand this subject, look around you.

How many trees do you see?

How many trees are there in your own garden?

How many plants do you have around you that give off oxygen to the environment?

How many trees do you plan to plant every year so that everyone on the planet can benefit in wellness and wellbeing? Take some time to consider these questions and act upon it. Nadhi Shodhana Pranayama practice helps to replenish and oxygenate both left and right side of your brain. It is a very good practice before the start of a shift, before an exam, or before a procedure.

## *How to practice*
## *Shodhana Pranayama*

1. Find a comfortable position sitting.
2. Take 3 normal breathes in through your nose and out through your mouth.
3. Now close your right nostril with your right thumb. Take a deep breathe through your left nostril.
4. Now close your left nostril with your ring finger and release your right thumb as you breathe out.
5. Repeat this process 10 times.

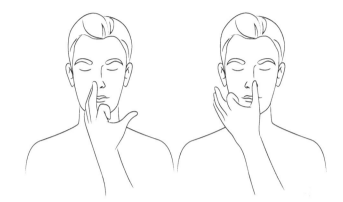

Illustration: Shodhana Pranayama

## *Mindfulness Meditation (Breathe Meditation)*

Mindfulness meditation is a practice that helps us fully focus on our present state and being fully conscious of our thoughts feelings and actions in order to increase wellbeing. Meditation is another daily mind detox process that is very easy and effective to practice every day. With the use of concentration and breath work we learn how to pay attention to our breathe as it goes in and out of our body , we learn to notice when our mind wanders and how to gently bring it back to focus on our breathing.

By regularly practicing this mindfulness meditation, we are learning how to focus and anchor ourselves in the present moment without judgement. We have to be very patient with ourselves and it can take a while to get used to this practice. So give yourself all the time it needs. When we meditate, we inject lasting benefits into our lives.

**How to practice:**

Find a quiet place , room, or corner. Focus on your breathing. This will help clear your mind of confusion and bring clarity of thoughts. Keep focusing on your breath as it moves in and out your body. If a thought comes then gently let it pass and take your focus back to your breathing. You can set a time limit as to how long you wish to do this mindfulness meditation. You can increase you time as you get comfortable with the process.

**Benefits:**

- lowers stress

- calms the mind and slows down body responses

- helps reset the biological clock

- Improves focus

- research has shown it to decreases inflammation and chronic illness

- reduce brain chatter

## *Mahamantra Chanting (mantra meditation)*

It is not easy to meditate and still the mind in the environment that we live in. By practicing Maha mantra chanting, research has proven it easier to concentrate and enter a state of calm using a mantra.

So, if you struggling with meditation, you might want to consider chanting instead to still the mind and enter a state of meditation.

Mantra chanting is a process by using a mantra and repeating it. One can use many mantras for bringing different benefits to our life. You can research the various mantras available. Each mantra has a vibration and needs to be pronounced correctly.

The most common mantra used is Aum. One can receive their own personal mantra too from a Guru, which can cost a lot of money. I use the Hare Krsna Mahamantra, which I find easy to use and is free of charge.

The Mahamamtra is:

*Hare Krishna Hare Krishna Krishna Krishna Hare Hare*

*Hare Rama Hare Rama Rama Rama Hare Hare*

We control the mind by focusing it with this spiritual sound vibration, which calms the mind.

When chanting the Mahamantra we are calling the universal energy. This mantra has many beneficial powers and is tried and tested. This mantra can be chanted or listened to. Both methods are beneficial.

I find using beads when chanting the mahamantra very helpful to stay focused as it helps you to keep count whilst your mind is occupied with the activity.

## *How to chant on beads*

There are 108 beads and one large bead.

Begin with the bead next to the large bead.

Gently roll between the thumb and middle finger of your right hand while chanting

Then move forward to the next bead and repeat the mantra

Continue chanting until you reach the head bead. This is known as one round and usually takes 6-10 minutes. You can gently increase your meditation time by increasing the number of rounds. Sixteen rounds is regarded as adequate for a good meditation.

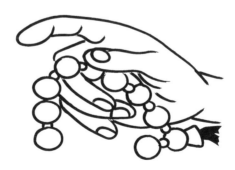

**Benefits:**

- frees one from anxiety and fears
- relief from misery
- brings happiness, peace, joy
- purifies yourself and your surrounding and those listening to your chanting
- dissolves negative thoughts
- cleanses the mind and heart of impurities
- enhances divine qualities of love, mercy and forgiveness
- a good method for those seeking self realisation

Dr Viveck Baluja, a neurologist at Henry Ford Hospital in Detroit, has conducted research on the effects of the Hare Krishna Maha-mantra on the brain.

The result showed that even in a resting state the brain is still not truly at rest. However, after chanting the Mahamantra the data showed almost no cortical or brain activity.

This is very interesting research for conscious wellbeing because it proved that you can actually calm down the brain by chanting. The above 10 steps might appear as many things to do in a day.

However, it is not all done at the same time. If you set a routine, you can accomplish everything within your routine. You can limit the duration of your routine according to how you want to design your routine.

## *Conscious Mind Detox*

It is of vital importance for you to take care of your mental health, as you would do for your physical health. I cannot emphasise this enough. Neglecting it can lead to severe psychological complications.

It is very easy to overlook a weakening of your mental health, as signs of deterioration in this area are not immediately noticeable. Just as you care for your physical health, you need to nurture and nourish your mental health.

The mind is a powerful tool that harbours memory. It can harbour past struggles for as long as you allow it. We can easily accumulate unhealthy lifestyle practices through the mind. Therefore, it is important to not only declutter your house but also to also regularly declutter your mind.

In order to examine what goes on in your mind, you first need to empty it of all other thoughts and then allow your thoughts to pass through naturally. You can make your routines more efficient and let go of habits or beliefs that no longer serve you. Belief systems that no longer serve you can clog up your mind. Make space for something new, reasonable and beneficial to your life.

The body is the window to your state of health. The body and mind are connected. A doctor is able to assess your wellness through several clinical tests that indicates the state of your body.

Wellbeing is a state of the mind, and you can assess it on a daily basis by checking in on yourself by how you feel. It can be done as regularly as you wish. Through the process of a mindful body scan, you can discover exactly how you feel.

A daily meditation is advised to maintain good mental health. Just before your meditation, you can perform a full body scan by checking how your body feels. Are there any aches or pains? Take notice of which parts of your body have those aches and pains. Evaluate your mood and your energy level; is it high or low? We are not meant to maintain a high-energy or good mood every day. Tune in to your body and mind and feel those energy levels. Do not judge them. Just observe and let it go.

It will change every day. There are many body scan meditations apps that you can download to help you navigate through your body and thoughts. These will work through all that is causing blockages. By regularly checking in on yourself and working through your blockages, it may help you free the blockages.

Just like you detox your body to rid it of toxins, you can rid your mind from toxins. Mental and emotional toxins can often go unnoticed and we can carry on with life not realising what we are storing in the subconscious mind.

It is only when we suffer some of the symptoms of stress, fatigue, indecision, unhappiness, lack of focus etc. then we take time to detox. It is not healthy and a lack of responsibility to yourself to avoid dealing with these situations until it presents itself. Take responsibility and deal with it as regularly as you can.

Most people declutter annually at New Year's where New Year resolutions are created for maintaining mental health. It's a good habit to form a routine for things you want to declutter daily, weekly, monthly and annually and not only at New Year. Here are a few ideas you may want to consider for your conscious wellbeing mind detox.

## *Daily Mind Detox*

Every day try to be mindful of the following:

- Avoid toxic situations

- Avoid toxic people

- Spend time in outdoor activities; try adding a daily walk to your routine

- Reduce social media time; Put your phone away after 9pm

- Take a soothing bath

- Meditate daily from as little as 10 minutes a day

- Reflect on your day's activities and things that bother you

- Journal entry your days activities and emotions, Observe the trends in your journals that you need to consider to act upon

- Nourish your mind with reading enjoyable books

- Play board games like Chess, Scrabble, Soduko for cognitive abilities of thought and reasoning.

## *Weekly Mind Detox*

Every week try to be mindful of the following

- Avoid Toxic environments

- Get rid of clutter around you

- Take classes of pottery, flower arrangement or whatever skills interest you

- Learn to cook a new recipe or bake a cake

- Set aside a me time day , treat yourself to a Spa

- Stop comparing yourself with others

- Keep technology out of your bedroom

- Take weekend breaks from TV, Netflix or your weekly favourite shows

- Delete toxic Apps on your phone

- Set aside "Worry days" and get in touch with all that is bothering you and find ways in how you will deal with it.

## *Monthly Mind detox*

Every month try to be mindful of the following

- Examine your diet and consider what changes you require

- Take time out to rethink your current job

- Meet up with friends or family whom you love being around. Set plans with them on how often you would like to meet up and what activities you can do together.

- Declutter your cupboard

- Clean out the old phone numbers of people you do not talk to

- Unfollow anyone who doesn't add anything positive to your life.

## *Annual Mind detox*

Once a year take time to be mindful of the following:

- Take a solo holiday

- Set your goals for the year

- Plan your activities for the year

## *Forgiveness*

As human beings, it is normal for us to make mistakes. As soon as we realise the impact of our actions, we can undo the mistake by apologising or through forgiveness.

Forgiveness is a very empowering act. Negative thoughts change the PH of our blood and make our bodies become more acidic and disease prone. If we do not forgive someone, we become chained and anchored, and this can debilitate our growth and expansion.

It can slow down every aspect of our life. By forgiving, we release the chains that bind us and set us free.

We are able to release anger, hurt, hatred, inner judgment, blame, victim mindset, animosity and allowing the past action to continuously play on our mind and keep us in the past rather than in the present moment. By forgiving someone, we do not let the other person of the hook. It frees us from the other person. Therefore, it sets us free. You generate healing. Forgiveness is the greatest access point of letting go of your colleague and allows you to move forward and practice to be in the present moment.

It sets you free. It give you a chance to start again. You generate healing. Life starts working for you instead of against you! Being trained as a nurse in South Africa I am very conscious of the fact that we are labelled "Mandela's Nurses". As South African nurses, it is something we are very proud of. For my generation of nurses we spent most of our school life fighting against apartheid.

When we won the battle, we learnt from our then president the art of forgiveness. Nelson Mandela said, "Forgiveness liberates the soul, it removes fear. That is why it is such a powerful weapon". Powerful healing lessons from a world class leader.

South African nurses are very sought after internationally for their hard work, high training standards and their ability to move on. Our hardships taught us many things. Forgiveness is in our blood and soul. It taught us how to be free. It taught us how to speak up without fear to make the world a better place to live.

## *Reflective Questions*

What is the most valuable message you received in this chapter?

_____

_____

What will you do different based on what you've learnt?

_____

_____

How will you ensure you do what you've written above in previous question?

_____

_____

What's been your light bulb moment whilst reading this chapter?

_____

_____

# *Notes*

_____

_____

_____

_____

_____

_____

_____

_____

_____

_____

_____

_____

_____

_____

# Chapter 7

# THE ART OF
# ALIGNMENT AND
# PLACEMENT

*"The better you feel, the more in
alignment you are."*

—Abraham Hicks

### *The Art of Placement*

Nursing is an art. The art of placement of items and objects around you can reveal a lot of what is going on inside your mind. A tidy bed space or workspace can reveal an organised mind. This is a feedback to yourself when you look around you. If your space is untidy then try to look into your meditation practice.

Is your meditation practice steady and regular? Look into your thoughts. Is your thoughts erratic and disorderly? Do you have lots on your mind? Are you doing too much chores in your personal life that it is reflective in the space around you? As soon as you sort out your mind, the space around you becomes orderly.

Remember it is possible to have organised chaos. Every colour carries a vibration. Colour is found in a rainbow. Through a spectrum of colours. There are colours from dark to light.

Be conscious of your choice of colours as each colour throws of an energy and mood that can affect you and people around you. For example, most of our hospitals are painted in pastel shades. Pastel shades help to calm the mind. Some hospitals are in pale green colour.

Green is the colour of the heart and represents the colour of love. When a person is exposed to this, they heal faster. Florence Nightingale taught us the importance of changing the bed linen of a patient regularly. Change of linen everyday not only is good for infection control but also renews the energy field for the patient. Dreams and thoughts carry energy that you cannot see. Just because you cannot see it, it does not mean it does not exist.

This energy can be dispersed on the linen. Hence, clairvoyants can give you a reading of someone by just holding their watch or handkerchief. Have you ever slept on freshly washed crisp sheets?

Can you remember what that actually feels like? Now you can understand what the patient feels like. The order in which items are placed around your patient reflects your state of mind.

The tidier and well-groomed a patient may look, the better your patient will feel and the better your mind will feel in providing this service. A good sight is a pleasant sight to all.

This also brings joy to the relatives knowing the patient is cared for. In busy areas like ITU, where there is vast amount of equipment, there can still be organised chaos.

## *Reflective Questions*

What is the most valuable message you received in this chapter?

_____

_____

What will you do different based on what you've learnt?

_____

_____

How will you ensure you do what you've written above in previous question?

_____

_____

What's been your light bulb moment whilst reading this chapter?

_____

_____

## Chapter 8

# CONSCIOUS WELL-BEING GAMES & CELEBRATIONS

One can play many games for improving wellbeing. Games not only help a team come together but also help each member to participate and develop observational skills

### *Shine Your Light –*
### *(A Game of Appreciation and Respect)*

Shine your light is a game played in teams to help make your team see positive traits in their colleagues. It is a game that helps to practice positive thinking.

## *How to play:*

This game is played by grouping people of a multidisciplinary team. They are given names of their team members at random who are not in their group. So you end up with groups of 5 or 10 people in a group. They are given some time to go away and think about one thing that makes a person shine from the list of names they are given.

They discuss it inter group. Then the most common trait becomes the one that they put forward. All the teams are requested to hand in their names at an agreed date. It's best to play this game during Xmas or Diwali.

The names of the person is written on the Candle or diya (diwali lamp), and their positive trait is written on the picture of the burning wick. This is then placed on the board for everyone to celebrate the teams' positive traits.

You will be surprised how many people have no idea how many wonderful talents they have.

This could then be celebrated with a dinner a party.

## *Benefits:*

- The advantage of this game is that it helps negative groups to focus on a positive traits.

- It helps to focus on a group members positive trait instead of only seeing a negative trait in someone.

- It helps reveal hidden talents

- It is suitable for areas that want to maintain positivity

- It adds entertainment in a working environment

## *You've Been Mugged – (A Game of Gratitude)*

You've been mugged is a very popular game to show appreciation and acts of kindness.

**How to play:**

A team member purchases a mug and fills
it up with goodies and a note of appreciation.
This mug is then placed on a team member's
workspace when the team member is unaware.
The team member now then has to purchase
a mug, fill it with goodies and passes it on to
another deserving member.

**Benefits:**

- platform to show and practice gratitude

- platform to receive gratitude

- Platform for colleagues to observe
  gratitude in action

## *Resignation Parties*

Celebrate resignation. Resignation means
it is time to start a new journey consciously.
It is very important to resign your job from
a peaceful place of being and making it a
conscious decision to learn from the past and
start anew. Resignation is a good place to begin
if you unhappy in your place of work or the type
of job you doing.

The universe is very kind to us and gives us many opportunities to renew our lives. It is a good opportunity for a second chance. It's our duty to wish our colleagues well so that they can move on to the next level of their journey.

Thank them for meeting you on your journey and the amazing things you learnt from each other. The more we happy with other peoples success, the more success comes our way.

## *Rewarding Success*

Celebrate success. Success is a blessing. Everybody loves a blessing. In order to receive a blessing, the secret is to be happy for other people's success. The minute you open your heart to receive this good news of success of others then your doors open too for opportunities of success.

Sadly we live in a world when we cannot hear or withstand someone else success. Many people cannot identify with success because they have not experienced it so they do not know how to be happy for you.

Forgive them and give them space to learn at a pace that's best for them. However, for those who know and experienced success, they know the secret and they know how to celebrate with you and be happy for you.

That is why the good old saying is hang around successful people and you too can become successful. Say a prayer of thanks.

### Journal your success.

Celebrate with others if you can and enjoy the energy of that success. Success ripples. Pass it on, share, and watch it come back to you. There is nothing like a success party.

## *Rewarding Failure*

Celebrate failure! Avoid a quick fix, it only allows you to feel good for a short time. Allow yourself to go through failure and deal with setbacks. Many people see failure as a loss. But failure to achieve something is a huge gain.

It is the experience of that failing which is a great reward. Nothing is ever done for nothing. There is always something to gain from every experience. If we hold on to the emotions of failure and not deal with it, it can present itself as a disease, which can become chronic if not released. Deal with the emotions.

Know it is good to fail. As the saying goes, it's in the valleys you grow. Nelson Mandela said, "The greatest glory in living lies not in never falling, but in rising every time we fall." From the process of failing, we gain:

- knowledge from that experience

- knowledge of oneself as a whole

- Knowledge of oneself from that experience

- Knowledge of other people

- Awareness of what not to do

- Bravery for an attempt

- Gratitude for being through that experience

Pat yourself on the back for your attempt. Journal your experience and all that you learned. Don't be hard on yourself for not achieving the desired outcome but be proud of your bravery for attempting.

Say a thank you prayer for inviting this situation into your life. Be grateful you survived!

## *Rest and Repair*

Our bodies have natural healing and detox mechanisms. We should not block its flow. If we change our perception, we change our environment and change how our body reacts to that environment. Anatomy and physiology taught us that our liver reacts to the environment through our mind without the liver even coming into direct contact with the environment.

This shows the vast power of our mind. If we regularly bring opportunities into our body, and mind to rest and repair, then we will be on the road to conscious wellbeing. Knowledge comes from listening. Answers come from silence.

## *Reflective Questions*

What is the most valuable message you received in this chapter?

_____

_____

What will you do different based on what you've learnt?

_____

_____

How will you ensure you do what you've written above in previous question?

_____

_____

What's been your light bulb moment whilst reading this chapter?

_____

_____

# *Notes*

Printed in Poland
by Amazon Fulfillment
Poland Sp. z o.o., Wrocław

53683819R00110